My Big
World

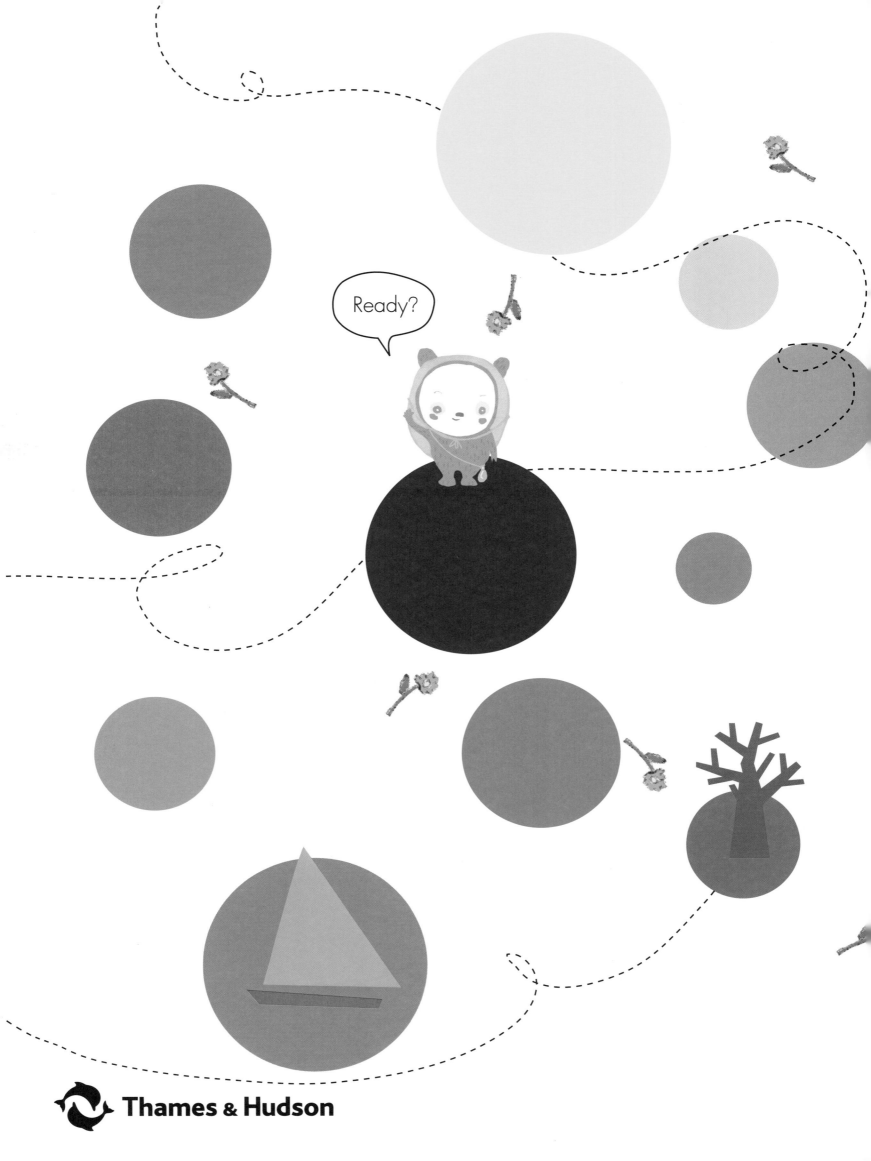

Where shall we go?

Let's go on a journey from home to outer space.

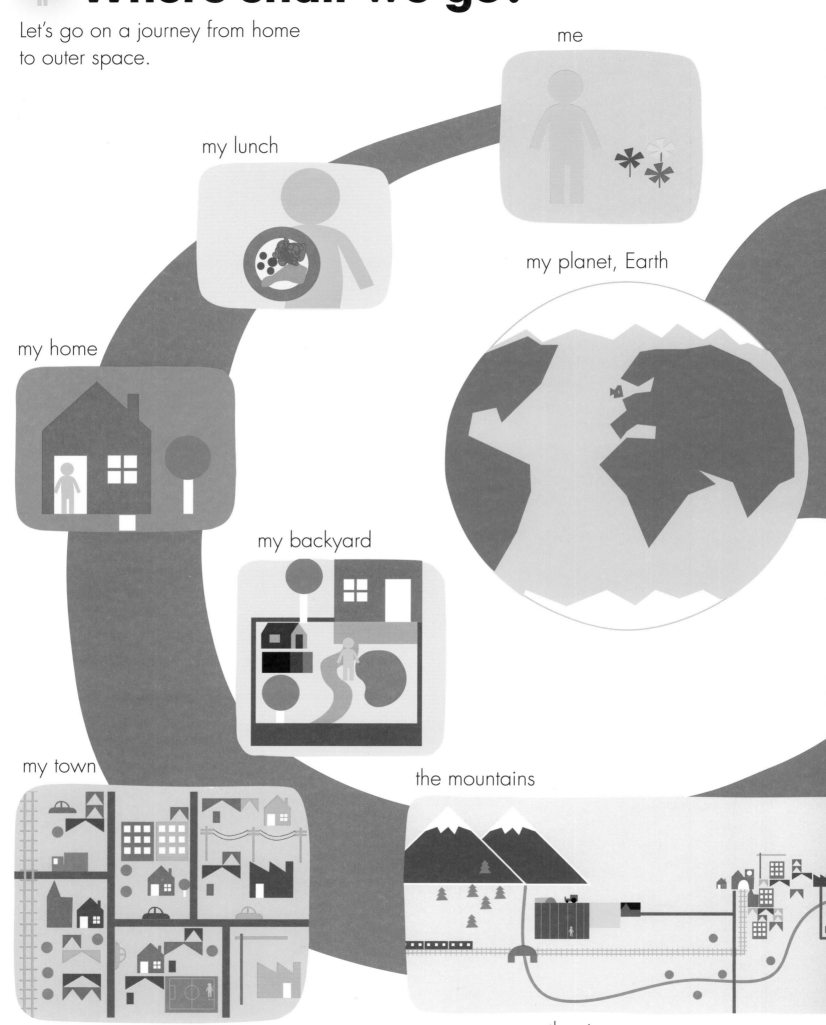

me

my lunch

my planet, Earth

my home

my backyard

my town

the mountains

the river

the night sky

the four seasons

the forest

the beach

Where to find out ...

How to use this book

Are you ready to go on a journey to explore the world around you? Along the way, you'll discover all kinds of facts. There are also fun games to play and lots of things to make and do.

Say hello to Koko

Hi, I'm Koko. I want to explore and discover new things about the world. Do you?

Hi, I'm Koko's friend Alex. Let's go exploring!

Did you know that the paper in this book is made from trees?

Where do you live? In a town or in the country?

When you see ...

... ask a grown-up
to help you.

... get ready
to do things.

Meet the explorers

The three explorers love nature. They are going
to show you what they discover about the world.

Follow me and
help look after
our planet!

I like animals.
Do you?

Hello! I love
growing things.

OK! Let's go ...

All about me

Hello, what's your name?

Do you have any brothers or sisters? What are their names? How many people are there in your family? Some families are big and some are small.

Meet the family

me

Mom

Grandpa is Dad's father.

Dad

Make a paper-chain family

Color your paper chain to look like your family.

Adult help needed!

You will need:

paper   scissors
pencil   tape

1 Fold the paper in half, then in half again.

2 Unfold the paper. Then fold it into a fan.

Grandma is
Dad's mom.

Uncle Dan is
Mom's brother.

Cousin Meg is
Uncle Dan's daughter.

Auntie Anne is
Dad's sister.

3 Draw a body with the arms going off the paper. Cut around the shape making sure the folds stay connected.

4 If you need more people, make another chain and use tape to join the arms.

Same but different

Read all the rhymes.
Can you spot which picture
shows which creature?
Can you find them all?

I have red hair,
Zack has black.
Sue has blue hair,
so does Jack.

Sue is spotty,
Steve is small.
Daphne is silly,
Tom is tall.

Flo is fast,
and Stan is slow.
John is giant,
look out below!

My lunch

What would you like to eat for lunch?

Does your tummy rumble when you're hungry? You need to eat. Food comes from living things, such as plants and animals.

Look at this plate. Can you guess where the different foods come from? Follow the dotted lines to find out.

Cows produce milk.

Milk can be made into butter, yoghurt and cheese.

Potatoes are cut and fried to make french fries.

Potatoes grow underground on a potato plant.

Peas grow in a pod on a pea plant.

cheese

french fries

peas

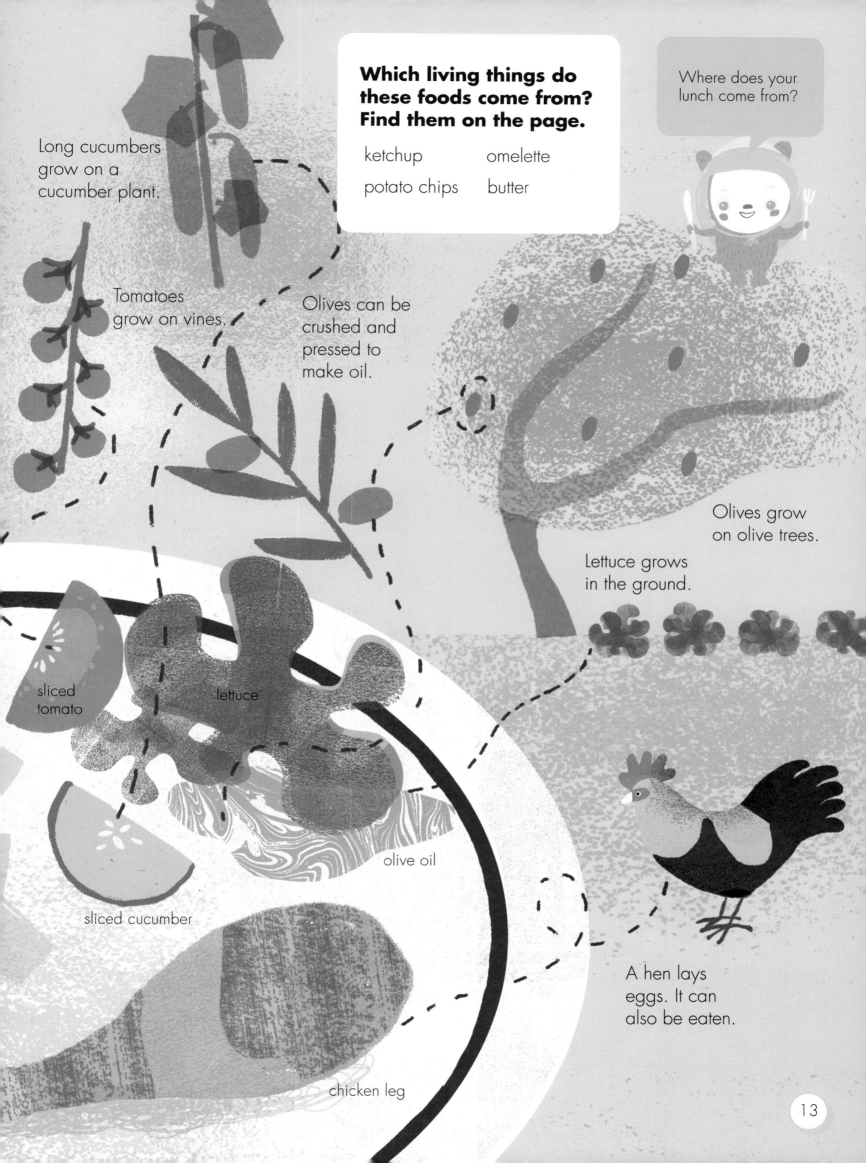

Long cucumbers grow on a cucumber plant.

Which living things do these foods come from? Find them on the page.

ketchup   omelette

potato chips   butter

Where does your lunch come from?

Tomatoes grow on vines.

Olives can be crushed and pressed to make oil.

Olives grow on olive trees.

Lettuce grows in the ground.

sliced tomato

lettuce

olive oil

sliced cucumber

A hen lays eggs. It can also be eaten.

chicken leg

13

 # It's time to eat

Guess what? Today you are going to prepare lunch. The best lunches are the ones you share with friends and family, so invite your guests and start cooking.

Adult help needed!

Make fruit kebabs

You will need

skewers and a selection of fruit, including melon, grapes, bananas, apples and kiwi

1. First wash your hands.

2. Ask an adult to help you cut the fruit into chunks that are roughly the same size.

3. With the pointed end of one skewer, thread on the chunks of fruit. One by one, add the different fruits. Make lots of fruit kebabs for your friends.

Make vegetable kebabs

You will need

skewers and cherry tomatoes, cucumber, cheddar cheese and olives

1. First wash your hands.

2. Cut the cucumber and cheese into chunks that are roughly the same size as the cherry tomatoes.

3. With the pointed end of one skewer, thread on a cherry tomato, cucumber, an olive and then some cheese. Make a vegetable kebab for each of your guests.

Make mini veggie burgers

You will need

1 cup of oats
½ cup of grated cheese
½ cup of water
1 grated zucchini
1 grated carrot
½ cup of corn
a pinch of salt
2 tbsp oil for frying

to make 5–6 burgers

1. First wash your hands. Mix all of the ingredients in a bowl, except for the oil and water.

2. Add the water and stir thoroughly with a wooden spoon.

3. Take a handful of the mixture and squash it into a burger shape. Put your burgers on a plate.

4. Ask an adult to heat the oil in the pan and fry the burgers for about 4–5 minutes on each side, until they are golden and crispy. Eat them with salad or in a bun.

My home

What color is your front door?
Do you live in an apartment or a house?

In your home, do you have different rooms for cooking, washing and sleeping? Look at the rooms in this house.

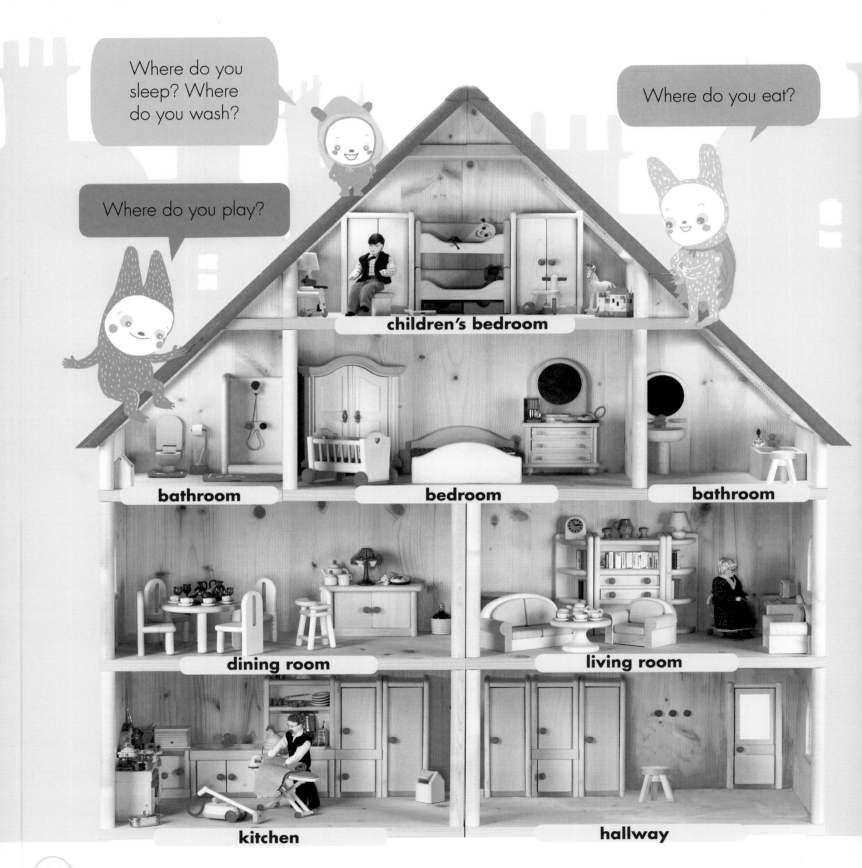

Where do you sleep? Where do you wash?

Where do you play?

Where do you eat?

children's bedroom

bathroom

bedroom

bathroom

dining room

living room

kitchen

hallway

Which room do these things belong in?

Can you spot ten differences between the two pictures of the house?

children's bedroom

bathroom

bedroom

bathroom

dining room

living room

kitchen

hallway

17

My backyard

Koko and Alex need your help to look for plants and animals.

Plants and animals are living things. Try to spot all the living things in this backyard.

Which kinds of vegetables is Alex growing?

Which animals live underground?

Which animals live in the trees and the sky?

Which animals live in the pond?

A good way to spot different plants and animals is to sit quietly and to draw them. Find a comfy spot outside, or inside by a window.

Look! The snail moved. It's an animal and it's alive. The stone is still. It can't eat or breathe or move. It's not alive.

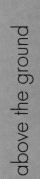

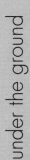

Build your own bird feeder

In winter, it's difficult for birds to find food. Help them by making this bird feeder.

Adult help needed!

Here is how to make a great bird feeder.

1 Take an empty plastic bottle and make two sets of hole on opposite sides.

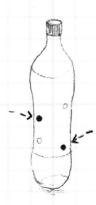

2 Push two wooden spoons through the holes. Fill the bottle with birdseed. Make the holes big enough so that seeds spill onto the spoon.

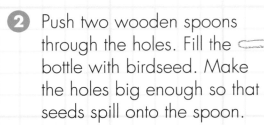

3 Make a hole in the cap. Thread a piece of string through it and tie a knot in the end.

4 Replace the cap. Hang the bird feeder in your backyard or from outside a window.

5 How many different kinds of bird come to eat the seeds?

You will need

a plastic bottle with a cap

string

two wooden spoons

scissors

birdseed

Make a mini garden

You will need

a big jar with a lid   *sand*   *charcoal*   *soil*   *moss*   *small plants*

Adult help needed!

  Add sand,

  add charcoal,

  add soil,

  add moss and plants,

… and perhaps add a few small toys. There you have it! Your very own **mini garden**.

This mini garden is like a tiny world.

When you close the lid, water given off by the plants collects on the sides of the jar and runs into the soil. The water is recycled round and round. When you leave the lid open, this water escapes, so you will need to water your mini garden.

Flower power

In this game, you are a bee with an important job!

Look at the busy bees flying from daisy to daisy, drinking nectar. Bees also collect pollen, which is a special powder that helps to make seeds. When a bee drops the pollen from one daisy onto another, a seed can form and a new flower can grow.

You will need

a die

a playing piece for each player

START

END

How to play

A game for two or more players.

1 Place your counters on START.

2 Take turns to roll the die.

3 The first person to reach the END is the winner.

Narrowly miss a hungry frog. Go back 3 spaces!

Different kind of flower. Miss a turn.

Bonus pollen! Have another turn.

On the farm

What's happening down on the farm?

Alex and Koko are helping out on the farm, where fresh food is produced. The animals and crops need to be looked after every day.

A windmill crushes wheat seeds to make flour for bread.

apple orchard

Help me to discover where these different foods come from. Follow the tracks to find out.

flour

bread

sausages

cheese

bacon

milk

eggs

apples

carrots

tomatoes

cabbage

Where does milk come from?

Hens lay eggs.

All the animals need fresh water to drink.

This is a wheat field. Wheat is used to make bread and pasta.

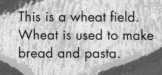

Cows eat grass. Milk comes from cows.

What am I spreading on this field?

We store hay in the barn.

vegetable patch

hay

Hay is grass that has been cut and dried. It is kept in the barn.

Horses eat hay. Where can I find the hay?

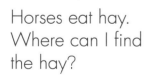

This is manure. Manure is animal poop! The farmer spreads it on fields to help plants grow.

Meat from pigs is called pork. It can be made into sausages.

Around town

Why is everyone going to town?

Beep! People rush into town to do all sorts of things. They go to school, work and stores. They walk, cycle, drive and take the bus or train.

Who's going where?

Find these little people on the picture map. Follow their routes with your finger. This key shows you what the small pictures stand for on the picture map.

key

school	
park	
shops	
museum	
swimming pool	
playground	
train and station	
bus and bus stop	
boat	
bicycle	
car	

27

Busy town game

How to play

A game for two or more players.

1 Take turns to roll the die and move around the board.

2 When you land on a light yellow space, miss a turn.

3 When you land on a bridge, roll again.

4 When you see a number on the board, move forward by that number.

5 The first one to reach FINISH is the winner.

You will need

a playing piece for each player
a die

START

+2

Walk in the park.

+2

ZOO! Miss a turn.

Bump into a friend.

SHOPS! Miss a turn.

Roll again!

Roll again!

MUSEUM! Miss a turn.

START AGAIN

FUN! Miss a turn.

Roll again!

LIBRARY! Miss a turn.

+4

+3

THEATER!
Miss a turn.

Eat an ice cream cone.

Roll again!

Go for a swim. **+1**

FINISH

Rivers and streams

How does a river grow? Where does it go?

Often, a river starts as a tiny trickle up in the mountain. Slowly the trickle grows into a stream. Then the stream grows into a big river that rushes toward the sea.

The source of a river is where it starts as a trickle.

A stream grows bigger and bigger.

A dam is a big strong wall that holds back water.

Boats travel up and down the river.

Let's cross the river at the bridge.

river basin

People use rivers for all kinds of things.

A town grows up near the bridge.

Adult help needed!

Sink the boat

An old juice carton makes a perfect boat. When you next have a bath, watch it float. Then try to sink it!

You will need

a clean empty juice carton

scissors

clean pebbles, stones or small plastic toys

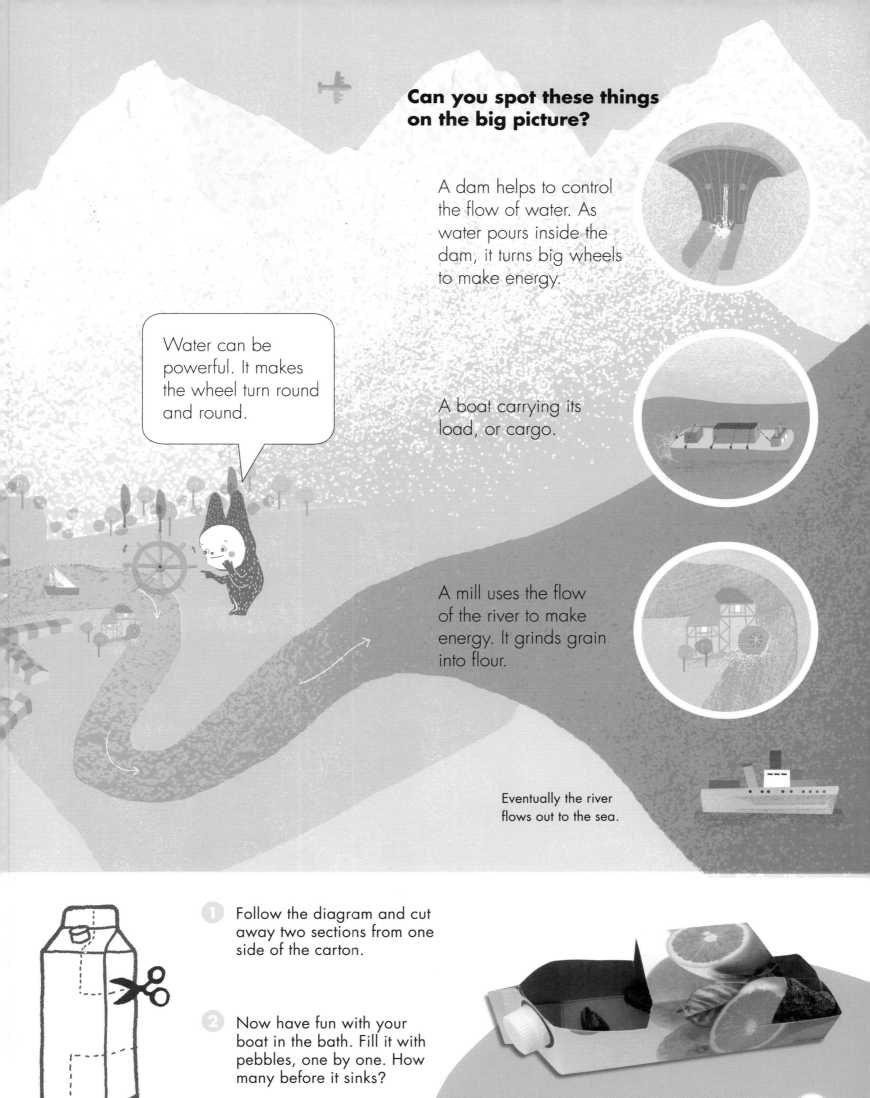

Can you spot these things on the big picture?

A dam helps to control the flow of water. As water pours inside the dam, it turns big wheels to make energy.

Water can be powerful. It makes the wheel turn round and round.

A boat carrying its load, or cargo.

A mill uses the flow of the river to make energy. It grinds grain into flour.

Eventually the river flows out to the sea.

1 Follow the diagram and cut away two sections from one side of the carton.

2 Now have fun with your boat in the bath. Fill it with pebbles, one by one. How many before it sinks?

At the beach

What happens where the land meets the sea?

The explorers are at the beach having fun, but soon the tide will come in and the sand will be covered with water.

A lighthouse flashes to show boats that land is nearby.

I'm a lifeguard. I make sure that swimmers are safe.

Why doesn't my boat float away?

I can feel the waves splashing over my feet.

What helps my boat sail across the water?

I need a snorkel to see under water. A fish doesn't.

It is often windy
at the beach.

I wonder what
I'll catch?

Make a pinwheel to spin on the beach

You will need

a 8 x 8 in. square piece of paper, a pin, a pencil with an eraser at one end

1 Fold the paper in half twice, so the opposite corners touch. Draw a dot in the middle and next to each corner.

2 Cut along the creases, but not all the way to the middle. Make a hole with a pin in each of the dots.

cut up to here

3 Bring the corners together at the center. Pin them together through all the holes.

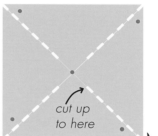

4 Carefully push the pin into the eraser.

Watch your pinwheel spin!

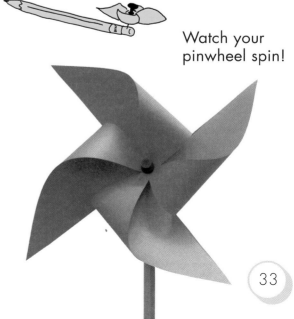

33

Forest adventure

Each type of tree has its own special shape of leaf and seed.

Can you spot the leaves that are in the wrong trees?

Bark protects the branches and trunk.

The trunk is covered in bark.

Roots suck up water from the soil.

Roots stop the tree from falling over.

Look! This seed spins as it falls.

A tiny seed can grow into a tall tree!

Name the trees

Use these pictures of leaves and seeds to help you name all the trees.

Deciduous trees lose their leaves in the winter.

 maple

 maple seed

 oak

 acorn

 horse chestnut

 conker

 ash

 ash seed

 elm

 elm seed

Evergreen trees keep their leaves in the winter.

 holly

 holly berry

pine

pine cone

35

Off to the woods

Ten things to do in the woods!

Next time you're in the woods or at the park with your family and friends, have fun trying these activities.

Adult help needed!

1 Make a den in the bushes or with sticks and leaves.

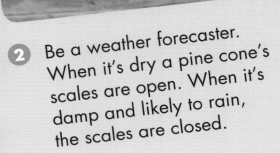

2 Be a weather forecaster. When it's dry a pine cone's scales are open. When it's damp and likely to rain, the scales are closed.

3 Play nut boats! Put plasticine in half a nutshell. Stick a twig through a paper sail into the plasticine. Ship ahoy!

4 How many different bugs can you find?

5 Spot faces on tree trunks. This one is smiling!

6 Collect leaves from different trees. Make sure the leaves are dry and press them between the pages of a heavy book.

7 Hug a tree with your friends. The older the tree, the bigger the trunk and the more friends you will need to reach round!

8 Make a nature trail with twig arrows. Lay a path to help others find your route.

9 Count the rings to find out the age of the tree. This tree was 18 years old.

10 Play hide-and-seek behind the trees. Count to twenty. Ready or not, here I come …

⛰ Mighty mountains

Get ready for a finger walk up in the mountains.

First, find START in the picture. Walk your fingers along the dotted line. Which animals do you meet along the way? Find out their names at the bottom of the page.

Only a few trees grow high up in the mountains.

A bear's fur coat keeps it warm.

Mountain animals are suited to living in the freezing cold.

FINISH

It gets colder higher up the mountain.

START

Find these animals in the picture.

 boar

 bee

 bear

 eagle

 marmot

 weasel

 ibex

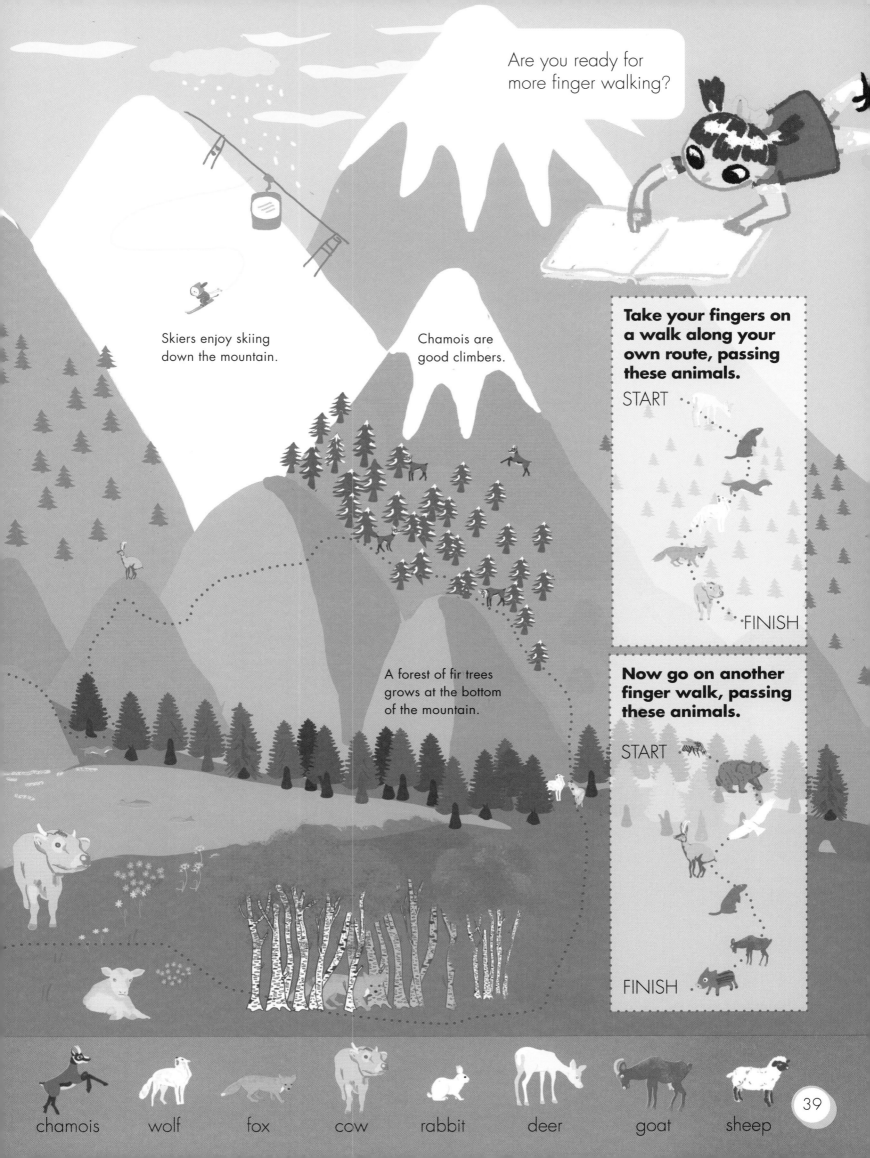

Are you ready for more finger walking?

Skiers enjoy skiing down the mountain.

Chamois are good climbers.

A forest of fir trees grows at the bottom of the mountain.

Take your fingers on a walk along your own route, passing these animals.

START

FINISH

Now go on another finger walk, passing these animals.

START

FINISH

chamois   wolf   fox   cow   rabbit   deer   goat   sheep

Hot and cold places

Are you ready to sing the hot-and-cold, around-the-world song? Let's go!

How to play

1 Gather together the following things.

scarf

sunglasses

gloves

hat

coat

2 Sing this song with Koko. Follow the actions, just like Koko does.

This morning when I woke up,
I decided to go around the world.

I packed my best coat,
sunglasses and a scarf,
my favorite hat
and a pair of gloves.

First I went to the North Pole.
It felt so cold!

Put your scarf on,
put your scarf on!

I saw polar bears and icebergs,
an arctic fox and husky dogs.

Put your gloves on,
put your gloves on!

Then I went to the rainforest.
It was hot and wet.

Take your gloves off,
take your gloves off!

I climbed up a beautiful tree,
and a parrot came with me.

Take your scarf off,
take your scarf off!

I opened up my arms,
and I flew away into the sky.

Put your hat on,
put your hat on!

When I landed in the desert,
I met a camel called Albert.

Take your hat off,
take your hat off!

Then I visited the South Pole.
It was colder than the North Pole.

Put your coat on,
put your coat on!

I came across blue whales swimming
and emperor penguins diving.

Put your scarf on,
put your scarf on!

When I arrived in Australia,
I met kangaroos and koalas.

Take your coat off,
take your scarf off!

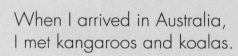

I had fun on a sunny beach and
tried scuba diving with the fish.

Put your sunglasses on,
put your sunglasses on!

When I came home at night,
I was so tired.

Take your sunglasses off,
take your sunglasses off!

There is so much to discover!
I can't wait to go around the world again.

Animal planet

Animals come in all shapes and sizes.

Different animals are suited to living in different places around the world. Match up the animals with their descriptions.

I don't have legs. I slide and slither around. I have scaly skin.

I have four legs, two big ears, long teeth and love eating carrots.

I swim in water with my flippers. I am black and white. I live where it is freezing cold.

I have eight long wriggly arms. I live underwater. I have two eyes.

I start life as a tadpole. I have two legs and can hop really high.

I live on land. I have a very long neck and can reach leaves in tall trees.

I am a big cat. I have stripes on my fur. I am a hunter.

I have four legs, spines on my back and can roll up into a ball.

I am the biggest animal on land. I am gray and have huge ears.

I live in the sea and scuttle on land. I have big pincers.

I live on land. I have four legs, a tail and a big shaggy mane.

I have wings, two legs, a beak and I am pink.

I have a curved shell. I move slowly. I eat leaves and fruit.

I look like a horse. I have black and white stripes and gallop.

I am tiny. I can fly. My wings are red with black dots.

Some animals in this picture haven't been described. What do they look like? How would you describe a monkey, a bat or a crocodile?

43

The animal choir

**Meow. Woof, woof. Grrr!
Animals can be noisy!**

Play animal choir. Do you know the sounds that
these animals make? Pick an animal and ask
a friend to make that sound. Then it's your turn.

 Ocean world

What lives in the ocean?

All kinds of wonderful sea creatures live in the ocean.
Ocean covers most of our planet. It is filled with sunlight
at the top, but the bottom is cold and dark.

Can you find
the treasure?

I'm swimming with a
blue whale. It blows
water out of a blowhole.
It's the largest animal in
the world.

Look, this jellyfish glows
in the dark!

This fish has a glowing
fishing rod on its head.
It lives in deep water.

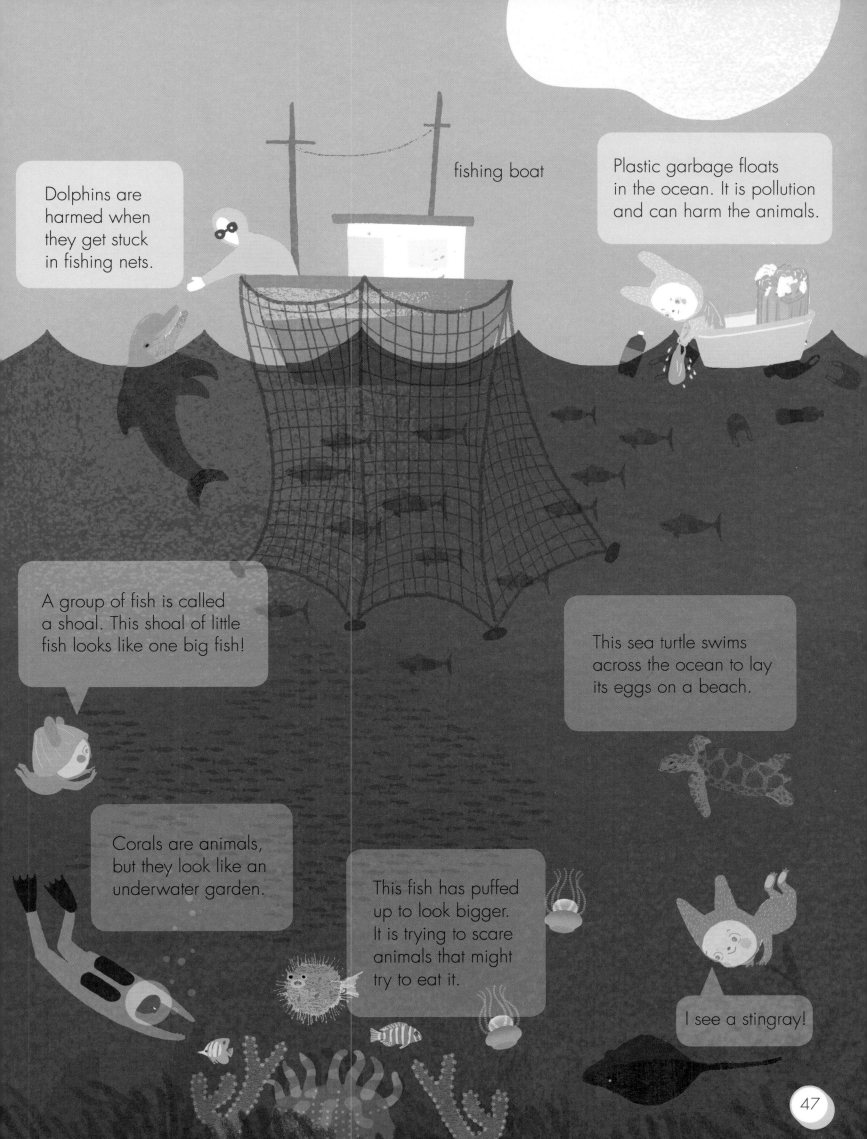

Dolphins are harmed when they get stuck in fishing nets.

fishing boat

Plastic garbage floats in the ocean. It is pollution and can harm the animals.

A group of fish is called a shoal. This shoal of little fish looks like one big fish!

This sea turtle swims across the ocean to lay its eggs on a beach.

Corals are animals, but they look like an underwater garden.

This fish has puffed up to look bigger. It is trying to scare animals that might try to eat it.

I see a stingray!

An island appears ...

Where did it come from?

Splash! Waves crash on to beaches all the way round the island. This is the story of how the island formed.

1 Long ago, deep below the ocean, red-hot rocks churned around. One day, they pushed right through the surface of the ocean.

2 They formed a volcano that spouted red-hot rocks into the sky. This is called lava.

3 When the volcano cooled, the lava became bare black rock. But how can trees grow on bare rock? How can animals live here? Where did those leaves floating on the sea come from?

During a storm, plants washed out to sea.

Lightning struck a coconut tree and it fell into the ocean.

The tree floated away.

Then the tree broke up. Can you see a lizard on the coconut?

4 The coconut and the lizard washed up on the bare rock island.

5 Soon, a coconut tree grew. Then grass began to grow around the tree.

6 After a while, more coconut trees grew and the lizard had babies.

7 People arrived to live on the island. They brought more plants and animals. They built a house out of wood. And they made a fire to cook food for their dinner.

Rain or shine

Quick! It's raining.

Where does all the rainwater go? Follow the explorers.

sun

cloud

1 When it rains, water falls from a cloud on to our umbrellas.

6 Drops of water collect to make a cloud. When the cloud is full, rain falls. Quick! It's raining again.

5 At sea, the water turns into an invisible gas called water vapor, which rises up into the sky. It cools and turns back into drops of water.

rainbow

2 Then the rainwater soaks into the ground.

ocean

3 Eventually the water appears again in a stream, which runs into a river.

river

4 Then the river runs into the sea.

Grow your own seedlings

Plants need sunshine and water to grow.

Adult help needed!

You will need

clear plastic food bags, dish cloth, stapler, different beans (including green beans, broad beans and runner beans), water.

1. First soak your beans in a glass of cold water overnight.

2. Cut a dish cloth to fit inside the plastic food bag.

3. Fix the dish cloth inside the plastic bag with a few staples in a line. Leave an inch at the bottom so the roots have room to grow.

4. Add water to the dish cloth. Then put four beans in the bag, resting them just above the staples.

5. Seal the bag and hang it near a sunny window. Watch the beans grow!

6. When the seedlings have leaves, they will need air to keep growing. Plant each seedling in a small pot of soil or outside in the ground.

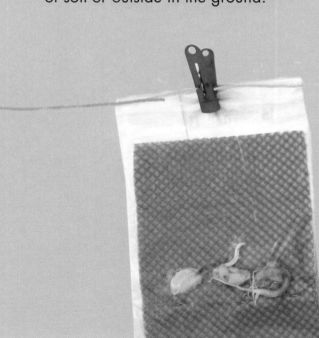
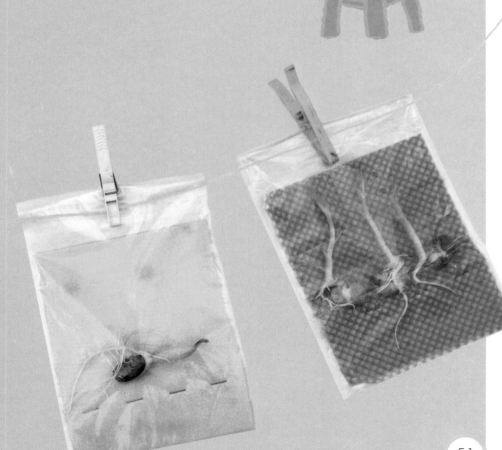

Whatever the weather

What is the weather like today? Turn the book around then read this out loud.

Jack Frost

run, run, run in the sun.

Shake, shake, shake in the big freeze,

There's a sparkling light when the snow is bright, and the day is full of fun!

So blow wind blow, stormy skies or falling snow.

Sun, rain and rainbow, will make the flowers grow!

Fly a kite when it's windy, wail, wail, wail, wail in the hail.

When the sky is blue, all your dreams can come true, and your plans will never fail!

Changing seasons

This island is magical. Spring, summer, autumn and winter are happening at the same time. Can you see plants and animals enjoying each season?

I spy

Play I spy with your friends.
Here are some animals to start you off …

Day and night

What happens when you're asleep in bed?

Some animals sleep during the day, but are awake at night. Other animals are awake during the daytime, but go to sleep at night.

Can you spot who is awake during the day?

Can you spot who is awake during the night?

🌍 Our amazing Earth

Where would you visit on planet Earth?

All of the places and animals in this book are on our planet. It's your big world to enjoy.

Where is it extremely cold?

Where is the train going?

What's on top of the mountain?

Where's the river going?

Where does a cactus grow?

Where's the cyclist going?

Where's the tractor?

This is our planet to share with animals, plants and each other. Please look after it with care and keep it beautiful for everybody.

Sun, Moon and stars

Can you spot any stars in the night sky?

A star is a huge ball of fire. The nearest star to Earth is the Sun. It shines brightly and keeps us warm.

Often, stars make shapes in the sky called constellations. Around the world, at different times, stars seem to make different shapes. Can you spot any where you live? Find your own made-up star shapes in the sky, too.

Let's do some stargazing.

Gemini

Hercules

Moon watching

The moon travels around the Earth about once a month. At night, look at the Moon. What shape is it?

crescent Moon

full Moon

new Moon

The whole Moon is always in the sky but often we can only see part of it, so it seems to change shape.

A satellite is a machine that travels around the Earth. It collects information about things such as the weather.

Cassiopeia

Virgo

The Great Bear

Leo

The Pole Star

The Little Bear

61

Make a cookie moon

You will need

| 1 cup of plain flour | ½ cup of soft butter | ¾ cup of brown sugar | 1 egg | 2 teaspoons of powdered ginger | a pinch of salt | different flavored jams |

1 First wash your hands. Mix together the butter, sugar, ginger and salt with a wooden spoon.

2 Whisk the egg. Stir it into the mixture. Add the flour a little at a time. Mix it all up to make a dough.

3 Knead the dough into a ball. Cover it with plastic wrap. Put it in the fridge for two hours.

4 Dust the rolling pin and table with flour. Roll the dough into a circle as thick as your little fingernail.

   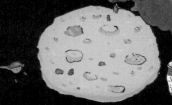

5 Cover with plastic wrap. Make craters with your fingers or round objects Remove the film.

6 Place the moon on a greased baking tray. Bake in a preheated oven for 15–20 minutes at 350°.

7 Let the moon cool. Fill the craters with jam. Now break the moon into pieces and eat it with friends!

Make a rocket panel

You will need

Cardboard from a cereal box, glue, paper, pencils, plastic lids, bottle tops and a round yoghurt pot

What to do

1 Glue the plastic tops to the cardboard to make buttons. The round yoghurt pot is your destination dial.

2 Draw stars and planets. Stick them to your control panel – just like in this photo.

3 You are ready to fly!

Hang your control panel by your bed. Set the destination dial and dream about your intergalactic journey.

Planet Earth is one of eight planets in our solar system. Where will you visit?

You are here

Sun | Mercury | Venus | Earth | Mars | Jupiter | Saturn | Uranus | Neptune

Index

Look up the names of things in your world and find out the pages they are on. Go through the alphabet to find the word you want.

Copyright © 2013 OKIDO
the arts and science magazine for kids
www.okido.co.uk

Photographs Copyright © Thames & Hudson Ltd, London, unless otherwise noted

All Rights Reserved. No part of this publication may be reproduced or transmitted in any form or by any means, electronic or mechanical, including photocopy, recording or any other information storage and retrieval system, without prior permission in writing from the publisher.

First published in 2013 in hardcover in the United States of America by Thames & Hudson Inc., 500 Fifth Avenue, New York, New York 10110

thamesandhudsonusa.com

Library of Congress Catalog Card Number 2012947782

ISBN 978-0-500-65016-5

Printed and bound in China through Asia Pacific Offset Ltd

Written by Dr. Sophie Dauvois
Illustration and Design by OKIDO Studio: Alex Barrow, Maggie Li and Rachel Ortas
Consultant: Barbara Taylor

Additional illustrations:
My backyard, Make a mini garden, On the farm, Around town, Forest adventure, Animal planet, An island appears, Whatever the weather, Our amazing earth and all the Kokos by Alex Barrow
Whatever the weather poem written by Gabby Dawnay
Cover design by Parusha Lewis
All about me, My lunch, My home, Build your own bird feeder, Rivers and streams, Hot and cold places, Grow your own seedlings, Ocean world, Rain or shine and Day and night by Maggie Li
Hot and cold places song by Marie Merlet
The animal choir and Changing seasons by Mathilde Nivet
Biscuit moon by Mathilde Nivet and Lily Monsaingeon
Same but different, At the beach, Mighty mountains, Sun, moon and stars and all the explorers by Rachel Ortas
Busy town game by Simon Pradinas
Flower power by Peter Slight

pp. 16–17: My home/doll's house photographs courtesy the V&A Museum of Childhood, London www.museumofchildhood.org.uk.
Puppenhaus, manufactured by Bodo Hennig, www.bodo-hennig.com